LOVE
and Marriage

LOVE
and Marriage

DAISY ASHFORD

ANGELA ASHFORD

Illustrated by Ralph Steadman

RUPERT HART-DAVIS
36 SOHO SQUARE LONDON WI
1965

Illustrations © Rupert Hart-Davis Ltd 1965
Text first published in
DAISY ASHFORD: HER BOOK 1920
This edition first published 1965
Second impression 1965
Rupert Hart-Davis Ltd
36 Soho Square London W1

Made and printed in Great Britain by
The Garden City Press Limited
Letchworth, Hertfordshire

CONTENTS

PREFACE

"A Short Story of Love and Marriage," I wrote at eight years old. It was dictated to my father, who took it down faithfully word for word. My very first story, "Mr Chapmer's Bride," which was also dictated, is among those that have been lost. "The True History of Leslie Woodcock" was a later production, and was written at about the age of eleven as a surprise for my mother on her birthday—it was originally entitled "The Q.I.B." (our family word for a secret)—but after the secret was out I changed the title.

My sister Angela's story, which she wrote at the age of eight, will certainly be voted the most amusing of this collection. It was the first she ever wrote, and it was followed by "Treacherous Mr Campbell"— another lost manuscript. A great deal of "The Jealous Governes" she wrote herself, as will be noticed by the spelling. Other portions were dictated to my father and mother, and I think the nurse had a hand at it too.

Since the publication of "The Young Visiters," I have often been asked if I don't myself think it funny. When I first discovered it—not having seen it since it was written—I certainly did. That is one of the most curious things about it—to be able to laugh at what one wrote in such solemn seriousness—and that is why I can never feel all the nice things that have been said about "The Young Visiters," are really due to me at all, but to a Daisy Ashford of so long ago that she seems almost another person. It has all been like a fairy tale, from the accidental finding of the original notebook to the day when, at her request, I left a copy with my friend Miss Margaret Mackenzie, for it is to her I really owe the publication of the book. She showed it to Mr Frank Swinnerton, and thus I was lucky enough to have it brought to the notice of Messrs Chatto & Windus.

But the real success of the book I owe to the great kindness of Sir James Barrie in writing such a wonderful preface, and I am glad to have this opportunity of thanking him publicly. His name gave "The Young Visiters" a send-off and a reading which it could not have gained on its own account, and of this fact I am most deeply appreciative.

DAISY ASHFORD

March, 1920

A Short Story of Love and Marriage

DAISY ASHFORD

LOVE

The house in which Mr and Mrs Molvern lived was one of the usual kind, with its red painted door and small garden looking out on a very dreamy park. The bed-room windows which all looked out on the front, had half dirty white curtains in them, above which could be seen dark silk sashes of the same dirtiness.

Mr Molvern was a red haired quick tempered gentleman, with very small grey eyes and a clever looking pink face. He would always wear brown suits, but as everybody said he looked much better in black. Mrs Molvern was quite on the contrary. She had indeed a quiet temper, with a pale delicate looking face with large brown eyes that looked at people with great interest, and her fair hair glistened in the sun. She usually wore half dirty white dresses, and in going out she wore a dark blue velvet jacket with black fur and a brown hat with red poppies. She never wore gloves except on Sundays and then she wore yellow cotton ones.

At the present time they had a young gentleman staying with them, who lived in the neighbourhood. He was sitting in his room waiting for the town clock to strike four, because when it did he had to go out and meet his truelove, whose name was Edith Plush. His own name was Thomas Henrick, but he was known as Burke in that family. At last hearing the hour strike, he snatched up a

felt hat, and putting it on his greasy head started off to meet his truelove.

When he reached Mionge Lane he met his pretty true-love skipping along most lady-like and primly. She was dressed in a light blue dress with a white sash tied at the side in two knots. Her long fair hair hung down her back tied with a pink ribbon, and her fringe was fluttering in the breeze. Behind her fringe she wore a wreath of green ivy. In one hand she carried a leghorn hat with red and blue ribbon, and in the other a silken bag filled with a threepenny bit and two biscuits, and her age was nine-teen.

"Well my pretty bird," she said as she approached Burke, "I hope you will like to 'manger' a biscuit with me" (I may add that she was fond of French).

"Thank you Edith," he said, "I will have one if it's a cracknell."

Then Edith burst into a fit of tears and howled out, "Oh, but they are Osbornes."

"Well to dry up those moist tears, I will eat one," said Burke.

"You dear!" said Edith like sunshine after rain, for the smiles had come on her face, as she opened her silken bag and popped one into his blistered hand. After this Burke and Edith walked along down the lane, which I forgot to say was shaded by trees all along.

"Burke," said Edith after a long pause, "you have talked often enough and said we shall be married one day, but when it is going to come off I am sure I don't know."

"Well my dear Edith you must recollect I am not a good dancer and have no nice suits, and you must recollect my people are not in this neighbourhood and I cant write marriage letters, and to begin with I don't

think my people would like me to be married just yet as I am not quite twenty nine."

"Well it is silly of you," said Edith, "after having talked to me so often about it, and bothered to come into my house, and sat on the drawing-room sofa to make arrangements, and now you seem not to care for it a bit, just because your people are not in the neighbourhood; and besides I was getting quite excited about it!"

"If you had only a little more reason in you," said Burke, "you might take it all in and understand a bit, but you are such a great stupid, so I must leave it alone and wait till I get a chance to speak to Mrs Molvern about it—she has got a bit of sense in her if you haven't," and his revengeful face made poor little Edith shudder. Indeed she was now too frightened to answer, and she kept on trying to go home every time she got the chance, but Burke's quick eye caught her every time.

Edith walked on slowly in front thinking what was the best way to cheer Burke out of his most moodful mind. At last she hit on a plan.

"Burke," she said, "I have painted such a pretty little tray, it will just hold a cup of tea and a plate of toast and the paint is quite dry now, if you will come in and have a cup of tea with me to-day, I will gladly show it to you."

This short but cheerful conversation of Edith's, made Burke quite forget their quarrel, and he turned round and said, "I will willingly come Edith, I know your good painting,—hark, there is four o'clock striking now."

"So it is," said Edith pulling her hat more over her fringe.

Burke and Edith walked down the quiet little village in which their houses stood. At last they arrived at Edith's house which was much prettier than Mrs Molvern's.

"Don't you think," said Burke as he advanced to it with

firm stride, "that you had better ring the bell, as you have a visitor with you?"

"Oh no," said Edith, "my mother would be sure to say if she knew it was I, that I was never to ring again, giving all that trouble to the servants; it isn't as if you were alone."

"Very well," said Burke, "I only thought perhaps it was best."

Edith smiled at him as she went up the front door steps. She led him into her pretty little bedroom to take off his things while she took off hers.

"How very comfortable all looks" said Burke, "I feel quite inclined to write a note at that pretty little table there."

"Oh indeed but you shant," said Edith just beginning her snappy temper, but Burke forgot to reply to her.

They then went down and had some tea and Burke much admired the pretty tray of Edith's. They had for tea some cold ham (the remainder of the luncheon) some toasted buns, a sago pudding, a dried bloater and a couple of shrimps.

After this Edith threatened to hate Burke if he would not arrange about the marriage.

"Look here, I wish you would talk of something else," said Burke, "I have a good mind not to marry you at all."

But at this Edith clung so wretchedly to his knees that he had to say, "well, to-morrow morning."

So that next morning Burke walked along down the village trying to make out where his own dear Edith could be.

Just as he was thinking of going up to her house he saw Norah Mackie and Evelyn Slattery coming along together.

"Your friend," they said chaffingly, "is picking some old geraniums in the front garden."

Burke stared at them straight and putting out his tongue once or twice, walked on to find his darling pet.

"I wish my sister Mary was here," echoed Evelyn, "she would soon strike out at you." And they walked on grumbling at his impudence.

2

MARRIAGE

"Well pretty dear," said Burke as he approached Edith's garden.

"Angel! I have been waiting for you to come and talk about the wedding."

"Yes I am perfectly settled," said Burke, and he began: "I have written to my people and they have written back to say yes I may marry you, and kind Mrs Molvern is having such a nice wedding suit made for me, and I think we will be prepared to receive the Sacrament of Matrimony next Thursday."

"Thank you so much," said Edith, "suppose we talk about it now here on this sunny bench."

Burke lifted up his coat tails and squatted himself down.

"The first thing to find out about," he said, "is about asking Father Fanty to marry us."

"Yes, now I have hit upon a plan this very minute," said Edith, "you will write a letter to him. I have got a rather crumpled bit of paper in my pocket, and as most men have got a pen in their pockets most likely you have got one."

"Indeed I have," said Burke, "and a threepenny blotter too."

As for ink, Edith had a halfpenny bottle in her pocket.

So Burke began like this:

"DEAR REV. FATHER FANTY,

I hope you kindness does not mind marrying us Miss Edith Plush and myself. We are both capable of recieving the Sacrament of Matrimony on Thursday next if quite convenient to you. Hoping you will excuse my craving for Matrimony.

Your sincerely,

THOMAS HENRICK"

Burke told Edith's maid to run to the Presbytery with the letter and wait for an answer. About a quarter of an hour afterwards this exquisite and most graceful letter came from Father Fanty.

"MOST DEAR T. HENRICK,

On Thursday I am free from all engagement and am most willing to marry you, and give a charming wedding breakfast in my lovely harmonium room. So with my best congratulations on your coming marriage.

I am,

Your affectionate priest

FATHER FANTY."

So on the following Thursday Burke and Edith were dressed as I shall mention now. The timid darling lady had on a most lovely sky blue coloured dress with a high bustle, and it was blossomed over with sham daisies tied on with green ribbon. On her head she wore a wreath of yellow roses, and her white veil reached down to the top of her stays. White kid gloves, and as the sleeves of her dress were rather short, her red beef coloured hands showed between. She had pretty white velvet boots with grass green buttons, and washed out red stockings. In her hand she held a bunch of green ivy.

The strong and bold bridegroom wore a red swallow-tailed coat, with a green silk sash tied in front. He had black knickerbockers and white woollen socks, and black dressing slippers, and he carried a bowler in his hand.

When they arrived at the church the marriage was splendid, but the bare legs of Burke were not much appreciated.

For the wedding breakfast they had several cups of Bouillon Fleet, and eight of Bovril. They had six Vanilla cream puddings and strawberry ices by the score; but they kept the blinds down in case vulgar little boys should loom in and say "give us a slice," while the leg of pork was being cut.

For their honeymoon, they went to the south of India, and seven hours after they got there they had two twin babies, a boy and a girl which they called Abraham and Sarah, because they were fond of those holy saints.

So we will say goodbye to this two chaptered story.

The True History of Leslie Woodcock

DAISY ASHFORD

TO

DEAREST MOTHER

FROM

DAISY ON HER BIRTHDAY

INTRODUCING THE FAMILY

"Sylvia Sylvia" cried a man's voice in the hall. "Where is that child?"

"Coming" answered the child for so she was always called by her Uncle Richard although in years she was close on 19.

And she turned to obey the summons, a deep flush mounted to her usually too pale cheeks, and lighted up her whole countenance.

Sylvia Monton was little more than a baby when her parents were both drowned whilst on their way to India where Captain Monton was to join his regiment. So little Sylvia was left an orphan and her mother's only brother Richard Earlsdown, came forward to take charge of her being a bachelor and possessing no children of his own.

At the time this story opens Sylvia was a tall thin girl with a fair and saddened face, which was only enlivened by the sky blue of her eyes—she had golden hair which she wore combed back from her white and noble forehead and arranged in heavy waves round her small and shapley head—a small rosebud mouth which when wide open displayed 2 rows of pearly white teeth. Small white hands adorned by 3 golden rings and a tiny round nose which she daintily touched now and again with a lace hanker-chief.

It was 3 o'clock on a dismal afternoon late in February

and the place was on the boarders of the Sussex downs.

"What a rainy day for our walk Uncle" sighed Sylvia as she approached her uncle who was still waiting in the hall.

"I wish it were finer my dear" said Mr Earlsdown opening a large umbrella manfully.

Mr Earlsdown was an elderly man between 50 and 60, he had iron grey hair and a long bushy beard to corrospond, sharp grey eyes and a would be handsome face but for a stern forbidding expression it habitually wore. He was broad and stout and had a manfull way of carelessly swinging his arms that gave him many friends. Not only this but he had a loud hearty voice that he knew how to use with a will.

Here Mr Earlsdown proceeded to turn up his trouser tips and offering a large umbrella to his niece cried in his hearty voice "let us brave the storm."

Just then a gust of wind blew Sylvia's dainty toque down a side street. "Oh uncle," she gasped dropping the gingham in her dismay "do go and fetch it," but ere she uttered the words a tall handsome fellow approached bearing his head and displaying the lost hat in his hand.

"Oh thank you" cried Sylvia a beautiful blush mounting her fair cheeks "I am so very grateful to you."

"I am afraid it is rather dusty," said the newcomer taking out a lovely silk handkerchief and preparing to wipe the charming object.

"Don't trouble sir" said Mr Earlsdown and taking out a large red kerchief he seized the hat in his huge hand and pounded it vigourously. "Oh uncle gently" cried Sylvia "you will spoil my feathers."

"I know what I am about my dear" said Mr Earlsdown "and you sir come and see us to-morrow, my child will be glad of a caller."

"Oh indeed I shall" cried Sylvia blushing.

And Leslie Woodcock, for that was the handsome

fellows name raised his hat and bowed low saying "I small be delighted my dear sir, but might I ask what your address is."

"Certainly my man" exclaimed Mr Earlsdown as with a hearty laugh he produced a little card on which was written

R. Earlsdown Esq,
Yellowflower Hall
Mayfield Sussex

Leslie bowed once more and taking the card moved gently away. What took place after this will be reserved for our next chapter.

LESLIE WOODCOCK

The hero of my story I will now describe.

Leslie Woodcock was about 6 feet in his stockings and fine and well built. He had very dark brown hair neatly parted at one side, a curly moustache of the same shade and deep brown eyes always half shut. He had a large straight nose and mouth to correspond, and white well shaped hands and feet, that set off this good looking young man.

It was about half past 3 oclock on the following afternoon when Leslie Woodcock, dressed in a light grey suit and crimson tie, black felt bowler and fur lined overcoat, started for Yellowflower Hall.

Sylvia, who had been expecting him all the morning was pleased to hear the front door bell ring, and hurried to the window to wave her hand, as she knew it *must* be the good looking stranger.

Just then the drawing room door was flung open and the butler announced Mr Woodcock.

"Oh good afternoon" said Sylvia rushing from the window to greet the visitor "how good of you to come in all this pouring rain."

"It was a bad day to come, but I was true to my word" answered our hero warmly shaking hands.

"Yes indeed how wet you must be" said Sylvia and

then turning to the butler she added "Johnson inform Mr Earlsdown that Mr Woodcock is here."

In about 3 minutes a heavy step was heard and Mr Earlsdown came bounding into the room laughing loudly.

"How do Mr Woodcock" he gasped between his peals of laughter. "I didn't at all expect you in fact I forgot all about you" and here he sank into a chair and offered a snuff box to his friend.

"Thanks" said Leslie stretching out his long thin fingers and taking a small pinch which he silently dropped on the floor as being so young he was afraid it would make him sick.

"You'll stop for tea won't you?" asked Sylvia arranging the folds of her green silk dress.

"Thank you I will if it is no trouble," said Leslie and a smile passed over his thin lips.

In a few moments Johnson and another footman brought in tea from the conservatory on a silver tray.

"Now Mr Woodcock please to help yourself" said Mr Earlsdown offering him three or four plates of sugar and other cakes. Leslie took a small jam wafer and proceeded to nibble it quietly. "How far did you come?" asked the girl as she was busy pouring out tea.

"Not very far" responded Leslie lifting his full brown eyes to her face. "I live in Astma House upon the high road.

"Oh I see" replied Sylvia with a nod of her fair head. "you have sisters and brothers then? for I have seen them coming in and out."

"I have two sisters and a cousin" replied Leslie.

"Oh what are their names?" asked Sylvia who had a very curious nature.

"My sisters are Violet and Hilda and my cousin is Albert Morris."

"*Oh* what sweet names" cried the girl "I wish you would bring them here some day."

"Perhaps I will" said Leslie "but Albert does not care for calling he is a very quiet fellow.

"I am sure I should like him, I love boys" said Sylvia.

Here Leslie thought he had better be going so taking his hat and gloves he shook hands after first promising to bring his family the next time he came.

3

THE BALL

About 3 months after the events recorded in our last chapter Mr Woodcock decided to give a ball in honour of his daughter Violets coming of age. So he sent out about 20 invitations and Leslie made quite sure that Sylvia was amongst the list of invited people.

At last the happy day arrived and as the carriages drew up in front of Astma House, Leslie's form might be seen standing on the door step looking out for when Sylvia would arrive. At last she came and Leslie offered his hand to help her up the steps.

Sylvia was attired in costly white satin with an edging of beaver round the skirt. The body was trimmed with real Venetian Point. Upon her hands she wore pink kid gloves and in her hair a pink may blossom. Her small well formed feet were clad in white high heeled shoes and silk stockings.

"I am afraid I am late Leslie" she said as she entered the hall "but I had such a bother to fix my hair, my maid was out you see" she added blushing.

"Oh never mind" said Leslie taking Sylvia's cloak and hanging it up "let us come into the drawing room and join in this walse."

Sylvia's programme was soon filed and she danced till she was tired and at last while resting in an arm chair she was not sorry to see Hilda Woodcock approaching her with a strawberry ice.

"Leslie is going to bring you some jelly or cream-pudding in a minute" she said handing Sylvia the tray.

In an instant Leslie came up to her and handing her a jelly retired quickly saying he would be back soon.

At that moment Sylvia felt a touch on her arm and looking round found herself face to face with Albert Morris, a short red haired young man about 22.

"Oh what is it?" cried Sylvia jumping up from her seat.

"Nothing much" replied Albert quietly "only as you are disingaged will you have a valse with me."

"I really can't," answered Sylvia hotly "I *am* so tired. I have been dancing all the evening."

"Very well" said Albert and he went away and Sylvia turning round saw Leslie sitting beside a young lady gently fanning her and talking to her.

An angry flush mounted to her fair cheeks and for a moment she could barely keep her temper, then without a minute's hesitation she walked boldly towards Leslie and his friend. Leslie jumped up when he saw her approach. "I was just coming to look for you Sylvia" he said and getting up he followed her to the end of the room.

"Who was that person I saw you talking to so loving-ly?" asked Sylvia.

"Oh that was Isobel May Saunders a great friend of mine" replied Leslie with a short laugh.

"So I should think a *great* friend" answered Sylvia angrily "and by the way you were talking to her I should think you were engaged to her."

"Look here Sylvia don't be angry" said Leslie slowly "but I *was* going to have made her my wife once but since I met you I have thought better of it—please don't say any more about it."

"Oh Leslie" cried Sylvia in surprise "but does the poor girl believe that you love her?"

"To tell you the truth Sylvia" replied Leslie, getting very red as he spoke "my belief is that Isobel thinks I love her and as I can not throw her over altogether that is why you saw me speaking to her just then."

"But what is your reason for not marrying her?" cried Sylvia.

"Well because I thought I would rather marry someone else" said Leslie, blushing and looking straight into her face.

"But who do you want to marry?" said Sylvia blushing in her turn.

"You dearest" he replied in an undertone "ever since the day I came to call upon your uncle I have set my heart on making you my wife. Do you think you love me enough to marry me?"

"I think I do Leslie" said Sylvia getting very hot "but I must speak to uncle about it first."

"Don't forget" said Leslie in a beseeching tone "and let me know as soon as possible."

So the whole of that evening Leslie and Sylvia kept together but as Leslie was helping Sylvia on with her cloak Sylvia saw Isobel Saunders gazing at Leslie with a look which went straight to her heart.

4

AFTER THE BALL

Before we go on any further we had better say a word about Isobel Saunders.

She was the only daughter of Colonel Saunders of the 159th who having lost a lot of money in the army was now in very poor circumstances. His wife had died five years previously and left him with three sons and a daughter. The eldest son William was a tall stout elderly man of about 25 who followed his father's profession. Robert the next was fair and delicate looking taking after his mother and lived very much at home and was just 21 years of age. The youngest son Frederick who was Isobel's junior by 4 years was still at school.

Isobel, who at the time my story opens had just attained the age of 20 years was 5 feet 3 inches in height, she had thick dark hair fashionably dressed and a massive fringe over her stately forehead. She had bewitching brown eyes from which long lashes swept her cheeks. She had an aqueline nose and a bright complextion. She had nice feet and was fairly podgy.

It was 10 o'clock on the morning after the ball when Colonal Saunders came into the breakfast room with an open letter in his hand.

"Here is some news for you Isobel" he said "Your aunt Miss Vickers intends favouring us with one of her weekly visits she will arrive this afternoon by the 3 o'clock train so mind and have everything ready or there will be a fine fuss."

"Oh dear" exclaimed Isobel preparing to pour out the whisky for her father. "I always dread Aunt Sophia's visits."

"Yes indeed she is an old nuisance but we must make the best of her and after all a week is not long."

"That is true" replied Isobel "but still it adds to my other troubles" and with a sigh she ran up to prepare the bedroom.

The town clock was striking 4 when a cab drew up at Vebena Villa and Isobel flew to open the front door.

"How are you, dear Aunt!" she exclaimed.

"Well my dear I am not as well as might be expected. I have had a severe cold and my servants have worried me so much that I thought a week's rest might do me good." answered the fidgety dame hastening into the drawing room and taking a seat she proceeded to give Isobel a list of all her complaints and when she had come to an end of them she turned to her niece saying "Please tell Jane to take my box up and then after I have had some tea I will go to bed I have had a long and fatiging journey."

Here will be a good time to explain Miss Vickers, she was tall and angular and thin with black hair, slightly grey which she wore in an untidy nob behind, she had dark piercing eyes that always seemed to find out other people's business.

Isobel smiled as the door closed on the tall and portly frame of her aunt and she began to re-arrange the room which already in ten minutes Miss Vickers had turned upside down.

5

AFTER THE BALL (CONTINUED)

Whilst this scene was taking place at Vebena Villa, a very different one was going on at Yellowflower Hall.

Whilst sitting at the breakfast table Sylvia Monton was wondering how to ask her uncle if she might come to terms with Leslie Woodcock.

Presently Mr Earlsdown rose from his chair and siezing his pipe he entered his study roaring 'Private Tommy Atkins' at the top of his voice.

"I am afraid my uncle is in one of his boistrous moods," sighed Sylvia finishing her coffee, "but he does get so excited poor uncle especially when he has been out the night before. I don't remember seeing much of him at the ball. I was so taken up with Leslie. I am rather glad I did not see him though for nothing would induce him to wear evening clothes or a shirt front and he insisted on going in his bicycling suit and such a soiled red tie and *oh* his hair it was really like a crows nest I don't know what Mr and Mrs Woodcock would have said if he had suddenly burst out with that dreadful 'Tommy Atkins,' but there poor uncle he *has* such spirits."

So saying Sylvia skipped into her uncle's study.

"Hullo hullo my lassie" he cried tossing down last week's 'Pick me up.'

"I wanted to speak to you Uncle" said Sylvia putting her trembling hand on Mr Earlsdown's shoulder.

"Talk away then" said Mr Earlsdown "I am prepared for the very worst news."

"It's nothing much" said the girl "only—

"Wake up wake up my child," said her uncle "only what?"

"Only that Leslie Woodcock has asked me to marry him and with your permission I will accept."

"I dare say you will" said Mr Earlsdown "but I am not going to give my consent" replied the excitable gentleman "I am not going to see you marry a begger."

"But uncle he is not a begger," cried Sylvia "he is well off, honest and dependable."

"I dare say he is all that" said Mr Earlsdown "dependable indeed! why ten to one when you have been married to him a month he will devoice you for some other girl he is silly enough to prefer; no no you shall marry a lord, that is what I want for my money, so next time you see young Woodcock just send him about his business, impudent young fellow!!"

"Uncle have *some* mercy" here burst from Sylvia's pale lips "I'll never marry any one else" and with a cry of "Leslie *my* Leslie" she fled from the room and flinging herself on her own bed gave way to bitter tears.

But finally taking heart of grace she siezed her blotting book and poured forth these heartrending words.

MY OWN

Owing to my merciless uncle I am forced to give you up as he thinks to marry a lord, but *no never*! my Leslie and although I may never see you again think of me always as I shall of you and believe me to be

Yours and yours alone

SYLVIA.

6

THE ELOPEMENT

It was past 2 o'clock before Leslie recieved Sylvia's wretched appeal.

It was brought to him in his room whilst dressing for an afternoon party. Leslie read it carefully through and then throwing it on the floor seezed his head in his hands and thought it over.

Presently he looked up with a determined expression on his face "I must marry her" he cried, and sitting down he picked up a sheet of writing paper and prepared to answer the note, and this was what he said—

MY BEST LOVED

If you will agree to this plan I will marry you yet. Have all your wants packed up this evening by 6 o'clock and we will elope together dearest and when we are one, we will go to America and make our fortunes.

Ever dearest
Your own LESLIE.

He then told one of the servants to take the above to Yellowflower Hall and give it into Miss Monton's hands, and wait for her answer.

The servant soon returned to say that the young lady would agree to the plan.

Leslie then began to collect his stockings and under garments and whilst rummaging in his wardrobe he heard something drop on the floor. He stooped to pick it up, it was a photograph of Isobel Saunders.

"Poor Isobel" murmured Leslie and wrapping the photo up he put it in his pocket. " I wonder what she will think of me when she knows."

At 5 o'clock the housemaid came to tell tea was ready.

"Oh bring me a cup of tea up here, I am not feeling very well" said Leslie as she closed the door.

At a $\frac{1}{4}$ to 6 Leslie slipped out by the back door. He was attired in a long old fashioned ulster, a deer-stalking cap, large golosha boots, and a hunting suit as he had gone to hunt for Sylvia. On his right arm he carried a bag containing clean under linen and other odds and ends also his money consisting of £40 in ready gold. He entered the garden of Yellowflower Hall and stole up unseen to Sylvia's room. He found her standing by the table buttoning her jacket with nervous trembling fingers.

"Oh Leslie!" she cried as he entered the room "I am so glad you have come" and saying this she fell back in a chair and fainted dead away.

Leslie caught hold of the water jug and wetting a sponge applied it to her white face and by this and the aid of smelling saults, Sylvia soon revived.

"I am so nervous" she said "Oh Leslie shall we ever get away in safety?"

"Yes dearest yes" whispered the lover, "trust me darling and you will be alright."

"I am ready now" said Sylvia in a weak voice as she put a packet of biscuits into her bundle.

"I'll carry your luggage" said Leslie picking up her bundle which was tied in a white tablecloth.

Sylvia had been more particular than Leslie as to her luggage. Besides all her underlinen she had with her two pairs of clean sheets and pillow-cases, some bath-towels and soap, likewise a sponge and a yard of flannel (in case she lost any) a flask of brandy some new potatoes and a tooth brush.

Sylvia's window opened into the lawn so it was easy to escape and once off the high road she and Leslie felt safe.

7

THE LODGINGS

Leslie and Sylvia having tramped until midnight found themselves weary and footsore at London.

"I can't afford very good lodgings" said Leslie "my money must last until I get employment."

"Where shall we go then?" said Sylvia.

"To some common lodging house" said Leslie "you see *you* have clean sheets if they are needful—ah there is the lodging house."

So he and Sylvia approached a filthy house at the end of a narrow street. Leslie knocked at the door and after waiting 10 minutes a dirty old woman with a candle in her hand, opened the door.

"What is it you want?" she said, "disturbing me at this time of night!"

"We have come for a lodging" said our hero "how much would it be?"

"4d a night single" said the old woman "and 2d extra if you want a drop of water to wash with."

Leslie's heart sank within him at these words but he felt bound to accept saying "I hope the beds and the water are clean."

"Clean enough I'm sure" said the old woman "considering they have only been used a few times." so saying she led them up a rickety stair case into a shabby little room.

"The bed ain't made yet" said Old Nan pointing to a heap of rags in the corner.

"Thank you" said Leslie and locking the door he turned to Sylvia who by this time was wandering hopelessly about the filthy garret.

"We'll make the bed anyhow" said Leslie "get out your sheets Sylvia."

She obeyed and Leslie kneeling on the floor began to sort out the rags. He found an old blanket which being a shade cleaner than the others he laid upon the floor covering it with a clean sheet; then stuffing his jacket inside the pillow case he made it into a pillow, he then laid another sheet over that and covered it with his and Sylvia's overcoats, he pronounced the bed made.

"How very dreadful!" gasped Sylvia "I can not sleep upon that bed."

"You must" said Leslie throwing open the window to air the room.

The next morning Leslie, who had sat by the open window all night began to collect the bed clothes and turning to Sylvia said "we will get out of this as soon as ever we can."

Then finding a drop of filthy water in a cracked basin he proceeded to wash his face and hands, though Sylvia said she would rather go dirty than use such water.

Just then Old Nan enterd and looking round said "well now I hope you have had a pleasant night."

"Oh very" stammered poor Leslie.

"I think we are going now, if you will tell me what it comes to."

"Well let me see" said Old Nan.

"2 beds and 2 washes—"

"But I did'nt wash" said Sylvia.

"And *I* did'nt go to bed" said Leslie.

"Then it will be *6d* growled Old Nan. and after paying their landlady Leslie and Sylvia fled for their lives.

8

THE MARRIAGE

"I wonder where we can find a church to be married in" said Sylvia

"We don't look as though we were *going* to be married" said Leslie "and I feel so soiled after sleeping in that lodging house."

"I should think you do" said Sylvia "I never felt so dirty in my life—why there is a church Leslie."

"Yes I know but I mean to buy you a white veil and a piece of lace" said Leslie "here is a shilling get what you can."

Sylvia hurried across the road and soon returned with a yard of book muslin for a veil and ½ a yard of furniture lace.

"That will do" said Leslie and they entered the church.

A middle aged man was busy lighting the church lamps and stared hopelessly as the people entered.

"Please are you the clergyman?" asked Leslie.

"No" said the man "Mr Roberts who is sorting surplices in the vestry is the parson."

"Can we speak to him" said Leslie quietly.

"Yes sir" replied the man opening the vestry door.

"Oh are you the clergyman?" said Leslie to a tall dark man who was just folding up some clean linen.

"Yes I am" replied the said gentleman "can I do anything for you?"

"Well we want to be married" said Leslie bashfully, "if this young lady may put her veil on in the vestry we could then wait in the church till you are at leisure."

"Yes I think I have time" said Mr Roberts glancing at his watch "please sign your names in this book and I will ring the bell for the acolyte."

So saying he touched a spring bell and very soon a small fair-haired boy appeared in the door way.

"Take two lighted candles into the church Tommy" said Mr Roberts "and place two kneeling chairs in the aisle."

Tommy obeyed and very soon Sylvia and Leslie were kneeling side by side in the church.

About 5 minutes afterwards our hero and heroine walked out husband and wife!!

"Let us have our wedding breakfast at the Gaiety restaurant" said Leslie and hailing a hansom the married couple stepped in.

"What would you like my dear" said Leslie sitting down at a ready laid table.

"I'd like rabbit pie and apple fritters and a cup of coffee please" said Sylvia throwing off her gloves and displaying her newly put on wedding ring.

"Very good my dear" said Leslie "and I will have a slice of roast pork and suet pudding and treacle and beer and soda mixed that is a mild B and S, my dear."

Half way through his pork Leslie pulled out a letter from his pocket and after piercing at it for two or three minutes he read as follows.

Homer Villa Margate

DEAR SIR

I shall be very pleased to acomodate you for a fortnight. You can have a good sized bedroom, parlour and dining room for 3 guineas per week including everything else. I shall expect you tonight so

Believe me to be

Yours very truly

MARY MASON

"This *is* good news my dear" said Leslie "if you have done your pie we will take the first train to Margate, hand me your bundle and we will start."

It was not a very long journey but Sylvia who was very tired was not sorry to hear the porters screaming "Margate station."

A pony cart from Homer Villa was waiting for them and Leslie and Sylvia were soon at their lodgings.

A fat good tempered looking woman showed them into a comfortable parlour where a lovely tea consisting of ham sandwiches, poached eggs, tea and bread and butter was waiting for them. And here we will leave them to enjoy it while we take the train back to Mayfield.

9

THE CONFUSION

About a $\frac{1}{4}$ to 8 o'clock the dressing bell at Yellowflower Hall pealed forth its usual summons.

"I am glad dinner is so nearly ready" said untidy Mr Earlsdown straightening his tie and running a comb through his hair "I'll go and have a quiet glass of claret while I am waiting—perhaps Sylvia will appear by then."

Mr Earlsdown had just drained his glass when Johnson brought in some pea soup, bacon and green cabbage, merangues and chocolate pudding.

"Don't trouble about ringing the second bell Johnson" said Mr Earlsdown "just call Miss Monton and I will begin."

So saying he began to serve out the bacon on a golden plate.

"Where is that child" said Mr Earlsdown after having 3 serves of the bacon.

Just then Johnson entered with a very long face "If you please sir" he said "Miss Monton is nowhere in the house and her room Mary says is that untidy you'd think a wild menagerie had been there."

"Bless my life" exclaimed Mr Earlsdown throwing down his fork and tossing his table napkin to the butler.

Forthwith he rushed upstairs to his niece's room and the sight which met his eyes was enough to astonish even Mr Earlsdown. A pile of linen stood in a corner of the room, hats, jackets and various articles of clothing were scattered in every direction and at last on the bed a letter adressed in Sylvia's hand to himself and this is what it said.

UNCLE,

Please do not worry yourself about me. I am quite safe under the charge of Leslie Woodcock. We shall be in London to-night but from that day forth I dont know where we shall be. My name from now is

SYLVIA WOODCOCK.

As Mr Earlsdown read this coldly worded epistle he flashed his eyes and stamped heavily on the floor.

"Why bless the girl" he screamed, "I'll have her back within an inch of her life" so saying he tore out of the bedroom and called for Johnson.

The butler came running upstairs to receive his orders.

"Johnson take the first train to London and search everywhere for traces of Mr and Mrs Woodcock" and handing the butler 2/6 he sent him off by the 8.8 to London.

Meanwhile there was also great confusion at Astmer House. On the summons to dinner Leslie was found missing.

"Dear me" exclaimed Mrs Woodcock jumping up and knocking over a soup tureen "Albert go and look for your cousin."

"Oh *he* is alright" answered Albert "there is no need to fuss."

"Yes there is you heartless boy, go and look for my son at once."

"Oh bother" said Albert flinging down his book.

"Dont snap" said Mrs Woodcock as Albert dashed furiously out of the room.

He returned within a $\frac{1}{4}$ of an hour to say he could find no traces of Leslie except his toothbrush in the back garden and a pocket handkerchief on the stairs.

"Oh I hope he is not lost" cried Mrs Woodcock "my dear son, where can he be?"

"Oh but you have me" said Albert with a faint smile.

"What do I care for you?" said Mrs Woodcock bitterly.

Albert immediately began shuffling about and took a drink of water to hide his blushes.

"As you are so *very* stupid" continued Mrs Woodcock "perhaps you can *manage* to walk as far as Yellowflower Hall and see if you can find any traces of Leslie."

Albert pushed on his hat and stamped out and returned in $\frac{1}{2}$ hour in a rather more excited mood than he went out.

"I say Aunt" he cried running into the dining room "would you blieve it just by that railing near Yellow-flower Hall I found Miss Monton's shoe and Leslie's watch key, I brought them both back to show it is true."

Mrs Woodcock uttered a terrified "Oh" and sank nearly unconscious on the sofa.

10

JOHNSON'S SEARCH

Johnson arrived in London at 25 minutes to ten. It was a dark foggy night and the air was cold. Johnson gave a shiver as he wrapped his ulster round him.

He wandered hopelessly about for an hour or two and oddly enough he took the very same lodgings as Sylvia and Leslie had spent their first night in London; being in that part of the city and too tired to look for better apartments.

Towards noon on the following day Johnson encountered a friend, Thomas Bench by name, and forgetting all about his errend, he turned into a public house close by to enjoy a quiet drink with his friend.

"What are you up here for Jim?" said Thomas Bench.

"Well" said Johnson, stirring up his hot whisky and water "it's rather a serious matter, my master's niece has gone and run away with her young man and I am on the look out for her."

"Aye aye" answered Bench scratching his oily head "what sort of a young miss is she eh?"

"Well she's a pretty sort of a girl with plenty of fair hair and blue eyes there is no mistaking she belongs to the upper ten my man."

"Oh indeed" replied Bench taking a piece of blue paper from his pocket "what is the young lady's name?"

"Miss Monton by your leave" roared the butler.

"Well" replied Bench, "look here." Johnson snatched the bit of crumpled paper and read it through. On the paper was written

Miss Sylvia Monton.   Homer Villa, Margate.

"Mercy" screamed Johnson "wherever did you find it?"

"Well" replied Thomas Bench "I was walking in Orange Alley where Old Nan lives and outside the door I found this scrap of paper, what do you think it means old pal?"

"I should say" said Johnson, biting his lips "it looks as though it meant that our young lady had taken up her abode there."

"So should I" said Bench with a broad grin and so saying the two men walked out arm in arm. Outside they parted and Johnson took the first train for Margate and whilst waiting at the station a telegram was brought to him by dirty old Nan.

Tearing it open he found it was from Mayfield saying that Mr Earlsdown was dying and he was wanted at once.

"Oh lor!" ejaculated the butler making a rush for the ticket office. Johnson did not arrive at Mayfield till 4 o'clock, then he instantly made his way to Mr Earlsdown's bedroom.

All the servants in the household were standing round the bed, and on it lay the unconcious figure of Mr Earlsdown.

"What is it?" cried Johnson pushing his way through the crowd.

"Appoplexy" answered Susan the housemaid holding her apron to her streaming eyes "the poor dear master was so excited thinking about Miss Monton and then all of a sudden he received a note telling of the engagement of

Mr Albert Woodcock with Miss Saunders and then that sent him off because he always wanted Mr Albert to marry Miss Monton, and when Mary went into the drawing room, there he was in a fit."

Just then the door opened and in walked Doctor Mason. The result of his visit will be seen later on.

11

SYLVIA'S RETURN

It was a beautiful morning about 3 or 4 days after our hero and heroine's arrival at Margate. Leslie was just finishing his coffee and toast and Sylvia was sitting near the window glancing over the morning paper.

Suddenly her rosy face turned deadly pale and the paper nearly dropped from her trembling fingers.

"What is it dearest?" asked Leslie placing his arm around her waist and kissing her pallid forehead, "has anything in the paper shaken your nerves?"

"Oh Leslie Leslie" shrieked Sylvia falling into his arms "read this and be satisfied that my nerves *are* shaken."

Leslie siezed the paper and read as follows:

"Mayfield Sussex. Last Tuesday Mr Richard George Earlsdown of Yellowflower Hall was siezed with appoplexy. On that same day he had prevented his niece from marrying a certain gentleman of the neighbourhood, and *she* has run away with her intended viz Mr Leslie Alexander Woodcock.

Mr Earlsdown is now repenting that his consent was not given to his heartless niece and that if she comes back before he dies, married or unmarried, she will receive his love and forgiveness for ever; he is now in a dying state and we fear that unless his niece soon returns he will decidedly expire."

"Shall you go home" asked Leslie quietly.

"Yes yes" exclaimed Sylvia "Oh Leslie, help me to pack, I feel too weak."

The trunks were soon packed and the heart broken couple were on their way to Mayfield. Arriving at the Hall Sylvia flew up to her uncle's room, and throwing herself on the floor shook the room with ear piercing sobs.

"Who is crying?" presently asked Mr Earlsdown.

"It is me uncle—your repentant niece."

Mr Earlsdown gave a contented smile and turned away his head. Presently he turned round and his eyes fell on Sylvia's white hand on the counterpane.

"Mrs Woodcock I see" he said with a smile looking at the golden wedding ring on Sylvia's third finger.

"Yes Uncle" said Sylvia in a low tone. "But you won't leave me till I am better will you child" said her uncle.

"Never uncle" said Sylvia, "never to your dying day."

12

HOW IT ENDED

Seven years have elapsed since the events told in our last chapter and our scene once more changes to the ball room at Asmer House. Leslie and Sylvia no longer newly married people are sitting by the piano and opposite to them on the sofa are Isobel Saunders and Albert Woodcock. Presently Albert advances to the piano and asks Sylvia to sing a song.

"Yes if I can get anyone to play my accompaniment" says Sylvia.

"I wish I could play" said Albert, rubbing his face and looking with sad eyes at Mrs Woodcock. Immediately Isobel seated herself at the piano and ran her fairy like fingers over the notes while Sylvia's melodious voice kept time to the music; and as the beautiful words of "See the conquering hero comes" rang out like a peal of thunder, Mr Earlsdown came bounding in.

Here the band struck up God save the Queen and everybody stood up in respectful silence; and as the last notes of the German band died away Mrs Woodcock took leave of her friends as we will do of the characters in this book.

THE END

The Jealous Governes or
The Granted Wish

ANGELA ASHFORD

WISHING

One evening late in Sep: Mr. Hose sat in his armchair reading a news paper. His wife sat in an other looking at the "Strand" Magerzine. Mr. Hose sudonly looked up at his wife; "Elizabeth" he said "one thing I have been wishing for, ever scince we were married is a baby, would you not like to have one looking at her seariously "Yes indeed I should" ansed his delicat wife with a sigh.

I soud like to adobt one continued Charlie, I would like to have one of my own said Elizabeth I don't like adopting babys, well you cant do it any other way if you don't get one. Besides if it was a boy what name have you got for it if it was a boy it should be named Charlie after you dear, and if it was a girl I suppose you would call it Elizabeth and liza for short would not you said Charlie, well yes she said beginning to read her magazine. Mr Hose now took out his watch and to his wife he said I have got to go out this evening at what time said Elizabeth at seven oclock I promised Mr. Lineap I would meat him at his offiace at a quarter past it is now half past 6 just half an hour. I have time to finsh this bit of newes in the paper, so saying he continued to read.

Presently the clock sturck a quarter past 7, oh goodnes I must fly, said Charlie Mr. Leanep will be expecting me he took up his boller banged it on his head took up a walking stick the first that came in to his hand, and

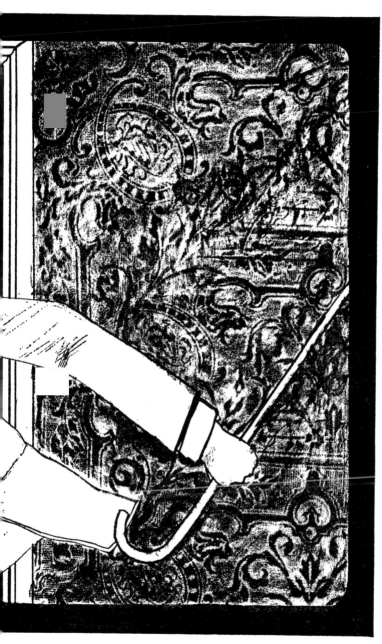

rushed out of the room looking like a roughyeun out of the streets, his boots untide his hair rough he banged the door behind him.

Noisie man mutterd his wife as soon as he had disapear. I feel ashamed realy I do nothing will keep him quiet when he has got an appointment never mind perhaps he cant help it she said and fell asleep in her armchair.

2

THE NEW BABY

Mr. Hose came back at about 12 o'clock he had drunken a little whiskey but it made no effect on him. He woke early the next morning and woke his wife and began telling her all about his evening stroll with Mr. Leanep but he did not say anything about the whiskey he had drunk feering it would shock her. But when the clock had just struck half past six they heard a ring at the door bell and within a few minutes the maid servant came hurrying up stairs and said the Dr. had arrived with a box under his arm and he would like to see Mrs. Hose she said. "Oh well, will you show him up to this bedroom" said Mrs. Hose turning to her husband and saying 'you don't mind him coming up, do you dear?" Mary went out of the room grinning, closing the door quietly behind her.

In a few minutes the Dr's bold step was heard at the door, and then a loud knock and with a "come in" from Mrs. Hose he entered the room.

"Oh I say Mrs. Hose" he began taking off his hat "I have heard you have been wishing for a baby, so I have brought you one and your wish is granted."

"Oh hurrah" said Mrs. Hose "Is it a boy or a girl?"

"Well I don't know" said the Dr. "*quite*, but I'll leave you to find out and settle matters" so saying Dr. Pauline took his departure shutting the door with his foot, while he held his precious top hat in his two hands.

As soon as the Dr. left the room, Mr. Hose began hurrahing and laughing at the idea of the new baby coming. "I am very glad it's come, arn't you?" he said to his wife.

"Yes, I'm very glad. Hasn't it come early?"

"Yes, said her husband, "but don't you think we had better open the box and look at it?" "Well perhaps we had," said his wife, cutting the string with a pair of scissors which were lying on the bed. Directly the box was opened, a dear little fat baby rolled out on to the eider down. "Oh, isn't it a darling?" said Mrs. Hose, sitting up in bed, and placing it between her and her husband; "What a pity it hasn't got its eyes open."

"Oh, but it's asleep," said Mr. Hose; "they never have their eyes open when they are asleep, except when they are very ill."

"Oh, yes, I see now it is asleep, it is blinking its eyelids."

"Hadn't we better be wrapping it up in something, it must be rather cold, poor little thing," he said, patting its face.

"Oh yes, of course we must," said his wife, jumping out of bed, never stopping to put on her dressing slippers, she walked over to the wardrobe.

She unlocked it with a small key she kept in her drawer, and on the third shelf she found a small, pale blue shawl, which she had had when she was a baby, and she had kept it ever since, in case she should have a baby when she was grown up.

"Here's the very thing," she said, "the shawl I had when I was a baby," she said, skipping back to bed.

"Oh yes, that's a nice shawl," said Mr. Hose, "and it's pretty big too, we can wrap it all round it; and you can cuddle it close to you, and then it would be warm, I should say."

Mr. Hose did not get up till half past eight oclock he could not stay in bed any later because he was already rather late getting up I expect I shall be late at my offace said Mr. Hose to himself buttning up the last button of his waistcoat, he then slipped on his coat put on his hat took up his walking stick and maid his apperance in the hall takeing a glance at him self in the glass as he passed it, he then opened the hall door and began walking at a quick pace to his offaice he was not so late after all.

3

THE BAPTISM

It was a lovely day on the 28th of september when a carriage drove up to the door and Mr. and Mrs. Hose with the baby in her arms ran down the door steps and into the carriage Mr. Hose doing the same. "It's a good thing its a nice day isn't it Charlie?" she said to her husband "Yes it is a good job or the baby couldn't have come out tho'. He isn't so very delicate, by the bye what's his name going to be?"

"Charles Edward" she said "Charles after you and Edward after his grandfather." "I hope Miss Gurling is at the church now, she's always late for everything,"

"She is going to be the godmother isn't she?" asked Charlie "Yes" said his wife "You don't object do you? And his godfather is that pious man who kneels before us in church, Mr. Johns."

"Oh he is a nice man that" said the father clapping his hands "I am glad he is going to be the godfather"

"Why here we are" said his wife jumping out of the carriage.

"Oh yes" said he stepping out with a laudable air.

"Oh dear" said his wife "I've left the baby in the carriage" "Oh poor thing" said the husband running back for it. Goodbye Tompson "said he to the coachman here's 6d for you, it's quite enough for him" he murmured to his wife as he took off his hat very reverently at the

church door. When they got into the church the first person they saw was Miss Gerling sitting quitertly in the bottem seat saying her prays very dovoutly. Mrs. Hose went up to her oh I say she began you are the godmother "Yes said Miss Gerling it is going to begin soon. what? said Mrs. Hose the christening said Miss Gerling Mr. Johns is not here we are wateing for him. Presently Father clocks came bussling down the church he went up to Mr. Hose and said "I can't think why Mr. Johns is not here he is very late, yes he is said Mr. Hose and the worst of it is we cant begin without him. No we cant said the preast it is a great nuisance he continued shacking his black head of hair. after about half an hour the church door opened and in came Mr. Jons he walked quite calmly up the aisle of the curch to his own seat, takeing it more as if he was very early insted of very late, he said a few prays and then he went down to the bottom of the church and said in a rather loud wisper had not we better begin yes said father clocks putting on his stoll.

All this while during the christening Mr. Johns kept standing on one leg and blowing his nose rather hard, he didn't have to say much tho he looked rather embarrassed. When it was all over they took their departure and went home in the carraige, but poor Mr. Hose parted with a good deal of his pence, because little boys kept running after his carriage and would not go away without a copper or so.

"As we are passing the confectioners" said Mr. Hose to his wife, "we might tell them to send up a nice sugar cake in honour of baby's Xning.

"Oh yes we might do that" said his wife, scratching her head to show off her net which was carefully covering her knob behind.

They arrived home at last and had the beautiful Xning cake between them for tea.

4

ENGAGING THE NURSERY GOVERNESS

"Do you know my dear" said Mr. Hose to his wife one morning at breakfast "what I was thinking of doing?" "No" said his wife looking very surprised, "What is it?"

"Well" he said "I was thinking of getting a nursery governess."

"A nursery Governess" said his wife, "Why the baby isn't old enough to have one yet, remember it's only 6 months old."

"Well" said Mr. Hose "I was thinking of getting one because only think to yourself how very useful she would be, she could help us in the evening when baby was in bed and besides that she could look after baby and he would get used to her before it was time to be taught."

"Oh yes" said his wife "now I see what you mean it would be a very good thing. You and I must go and see Madam Toinette about one in London tomorrow."

When breakfast was over, they went into the drawing room and Mrs. H began knitting a pr. of socks for her short coated boy, and her husband curled himself up in an arm chair and smoked to a low degree.

"I say Lizzie eh! why shouldn't we go to London today eh?" (he was rather a cockney man.)

"Yes we can go today, I don't see what harm it could do. We'll go in the afternoon then."

"Right you are," said the husband, "I'll change my clothes" he said as he retired to his bedroom and his wife continued to knit the pair of socks she was knitting for her baby.

Presently just after the dinner-bell had rung, down came Mr. Hose from his bedroom looking like a duke instead of a mere Mr.

"I say wife do you think I look nice. I have been such a long time dressing do you know what I've put on clean?"

"No said his wife who did not take the least interest in a man's toilet. Well he said clearing his throat and pulling up his trousers and sitting down. "I've put on this beautiful black suit with coat tails and a lovely clean shirt he said stroking his front and I've put on a clean pair of scarlet socks with a hole in but it does not show and he continued I've got on a nice pair of black trousers but he said with a sorrowful face the button has come off from my trousers which makes one leg shorter than the other. This being the only sentence his wife had heard she looked up from her plate and said "Oh you poor dear! never mind I'll sew it on for you after dinner. "Oh thank you so much! said Mr. Hose I should not have been able to go to London if you had not thought of this kind offer. Now Charles said his wife eat your dinner because we are going by the 3.15 train. Charles began eating his dinner quickly saying at the same time with his mouth full "Do you think baby will be all right with the housemaid.

"Oh yes he will be all right it is only for a few howers" said Mrs. Hose.

"Oh yes" said Mr. Hose beginning to eat his dinner.

Presently his wife looked up and said now Charles, I have done my dinner and I am going up to get ready and she went out of the room.

Mr. Hose finnished his dinner and then put on his top hat and took his best cherry wood walking stick. He could not see his wife anywhere; so like a wise man he began walking down to the station when he was half way whom should be see but his wife walking sedately along; she looked very nice in a coffee coloured dress trimmed with brown velvet a bonnet to match with a pretty bird in front and strings of brown velvet as well as a large bow of the same; she had brown gloves and a pretty light coffee coloured parasol in her hands, her nice walking shoes and stockings just peeped from under her dress. Well said Charlie we are not late for the train."

"An't we" said his wife looking at her watch which she wore on her bracelet. "No" said Charlie but you do look nice.

They arrived at the station and jumped into a first class class carriage.

Presently they arrived in London and walked arm in arm from the station. They walked up to Madame Antoinette's house to ask if she knew of any governess which they could engage. A nice fat looking servant answered the door. Is Madame Antoinette at home. Yes mam' she said looking rather ignorant will you step this way. (Mrs. Hose walked into the drawing room and sat down waiting for Madame Antoinette) Presently Madame Antoinette came down into the room. Good morning Mrs. Hose she said. Oh good morning Madame Antoinette said Mrs. Hose sit down but do you know of any governesses which we could engage? Well said Madame Antoinette frowning there is a Miss Brentnor she lives in Julian Road No. 36. Oh what is she like? Oh she has fair hair at least you may say carrotty hair and one good thing about her is her eyes she has lovely big grey eyes. She has a very sallow complexion and she had a blue dress on last time I saw her.

Do you know of any other governesses continued Mr. Hose? Yes said Madame Antoinette there is a very nice young lady called Miss Smith she has dark hair and brown eyes but she is rather cow-like she has rather boisterous feet and a few freckles on the top of her nose but she is all right you know and she lives in Buttonbrick House Hudson's Street and then there is another young lady called Miss Junick. She left her last place and was hated in this family and I have been told that she was known to take a few things that did not belong to her in that house; but I can scarcely believe that for she is a beautiful young lady and I like her very much. They left Madame Antoinette's house and went to call on Miss Brentnor and Miss Smith but did not like either of them. They went home and the next morning a letter came addressed to Mrs. Hose and she opened it and this is what she read

MADAM

I beg to present you with the photograph which you ask me to send. I think I have very good features and I *know* I'll make a excellent governess. It is not at all true what was said about me in my last situation and I am willing to come and look after your little boy and teach him when he is old enough. Give me a nice bedroom Madam; of course I am a Catholic which I suppose you heard from Madame Antoinette.

I remain Yours truly,

ROSE M. JUNICK.

Mrs. Hose answered the letter and this is what she put,

DEAR MISS JUNICK,

I like you very much but I must not believe what was said about you in your last situation. Will you meet me at the Victoria Station on Thursday at half past four and I will ask you a few questions.

Yours truly,

E. HOSE.

Mrs. Hose was now satisfied she'd answered the letter and in time she would have the governess with her.

THE GOVERNES ARRIVES

The next morning Mrs. Hose ordered breakfast early than usual in order that she might get off by the 9/30 becaus she was going to do a little shoping first and she thought to her self she could get a beautiful dinner at one of the Resteraunts and she smacked her lips as she sat down to her breakfast of eggs and beacon and a cup of cocoa. When she had finished she went up stairs and placed her bonnet on her head and buttoned up her patent leather boots and took an umbrella because it looked stormy and started on her way to the station bidding her husband farewell.

Directly she got outside it began to rain so she put up umbrela and within ten minets she got to the station and jumped into a first class carriage (for she licked to look grand) and soon the train started off for the smokey and dreary city.

At last the train got to Victora and out jumped Mrs. hose without a moments delay, she walked up and down outside the refreshment room (for this was where she was to meet our Heroine) she went up to one lady and said do you mind me asking you but I am looking for my future governess Miss Junick do you posess that name I am sorry for your sake that I do not she answerd politely and walked on. then Mrs. hose asked another lady who was peradeing up and down in a red and gray dress eating a halfpeny bun which she had just bought. Mrs. Hose

advanced towards her and when she got close to her she
saw she was very pretty so she thorght she would be as
polite as she could and began have I the pleasure of
meeting Miss Junick. I am not Miss Junick but I am a
friend of the dear ladys (best luck) and she told me she
would be here to meet you at half past four this afternoon
oh thank you said Mrs. Hose I now recerlect I was thinking I had to meet her this morning farewell or a deiw
as the french say she said as she left the station to go and
get some dinner. Perhaps you would like to know what
she had for dinner—rabbit and mérangues were what she
chose and she drank sherry wine. After dinner she went
into the depth of London to look at some of the shops and
came back in time to see the governess. As she entered
Victoria station she met a precise young lady hastening
to the refreshment room, she hurried after her and when she
got up to her thought she looked like Miss Junick in the
face, but before she could say a word the lady jumped
sideways and asked her was she Mrs. Hose and with an
answer of yes they walked together into the waiting room
and sat down upon a horse hair cushion and they now
commenced their conversation.

"How long were you in your last place?"

"Two years madam'

"Oh and was that yourfrst place?"

"Oh no I was abroad before with three french children
there was only one in the other family and she was a
throro' English child—so was her mother."

"Oh and what do you teach", said Mrs. Hose cocking
up one eyebrow.

"Music, drawing, the use of the globes, etc., etc. only
you don't want me to teach your little boy yet do you?"

"No, no, no," said Mrs. Hose "not yet he is only 6
months old, but are you very fond of children and have
you any little sisters and brothers?"

"I have one little sister of 10 and a little baby brother and I have two grown uppers, but I am very fond of children and wish I had one of my own."

"You won't whip my baby will you?" said Mrs. Hose.

"Oh dear no" she answered I'de spoil him more likely than whip him."

"Oh well I want you to be medium with him" said Mrs. Hose.

"Quite so Madam I understand babies thoroughly; are there any more questions you think you would like to ask me whilst I'm here?"

"I think I've asked you pretty nearly all she answered" except when could you come to me?"

"I can come on Monday Madam I was packing a few of my things in case you would have me."

"Let me see now" said Mrs. Hose pausing "how about the washing shall you pay it or will I?"

"Well I'm not very rich Madam and it would be a charity if you will pay it."

"Certainly I will and how much are you used to getting a year?"

"Either 5 or 14 pounds according to what I have to do. I don't do much for 5."

"All right I will give you 14. I hope you will do a great deal for that as I want you to bath the baby and have utter charge of him. And as you are coming on Monday, I will prepare you a nice bedroom" "Thank you very much Madam" said Miss Junick getting up smiling. "Good afternoon Madam she said hurrying out of the waiting room. Mrs. Hose came home by the 6 o'clock train and told her husband all about Miss Junick and Mr. Hose said he thought she'd do very nicely.

Monday soon came and with it the governess in a station cab and a large box with R.M.J. in red enamel on it. "Here I am Mrs. Hose" she said stepping out of the cab "who tips the cabman you or I?" "The Butler" replied Mrs. Hose he has a few shillings in his pocket— Come on John and give the Cabman 2/6". The Butler obeyed and helped the honest cabman in with the box. Miss Junick was then shown up to her bedroom to take off her hat. Then she went into the nursery and found her pupil sitting in a high chair all alone playing with his rattle.

Just the kind of baby I shall get jelous of she thought.

6

HOW MISS JUNICK'S JEALOUSY BEGAN

As she entered the room the baby looked up from his play, and stared at her rather hard, surprised at seeing a strange lady.

But Miss Junick did not take any notice of the baby's astonishment, but merely walked straight over to it, lifted it up, and kissed it a great many times, saying as she did so,

"Oh you dear little thing! how I would long to have you for my own." She then rang the bell for dinner, as it was then one o'clock, and she knew that she had to give the baby its dinner in the nursery. Presently the housemaid came up, bearing a tray in her hand with the dinner on it. Miss Junick then gave the baby its dinner, and got up and tried to amuse it, but the baby got cross and tired, not being used to her; so that she was obliged to lay it down in its cradle for its afternoon sleep, while she herself went upstairs to unpack her box. When she had done unpacking she came down again to see if the baby had awoke.

It was just beginning to wake up as she entered the room. She was pleased to see that it was awake, and lifted it out of its cradle, kissing it and repeating the same words as before.

At last tea time came, and pretty soon after tea Miss Junick took the baby in her arms and took it down stairs to say good night to Mr. and Mrs. Hose.

She then brought it upstairs again, took it into its mother's bedroom, and began to undress it. She found its little nightgown in a white case with C.H. in pale blue letters on it. The nightgown was very pretty, It was of white flannel, and the frills round the neck and sleeves were of pale blue, as the baby was dedicated to Our Lady of Victories.

When it was in bed, after kissing it a great many times, she turned out the gas and retired to her bedroom, saying as she did so, "I could never find a baby like that anywhere, not even if I were to search the wide wide world."

"Well! I dont know though," she said to herself as she sat down on the bed, "I might go out tonight, and ask the Doctor where Mrs. Hose got her *lovely* baby from. Oh no though, perhaps I couldn't, as I should have to tell Mrs. Hose that I was going out and what I was going out for. But I could pretend to her that I was going out to buy some Beechams Pills or a reel of cotton to mend some of my linen. Yes, of course I could do that."

And so, without a moments delay, she marched downstairs and into the drawing room.

"Oh please Mrs. Hose," she began, "I would like to go down the town to buy a box of Beecham's Pills, may I go?, she added.

"A box of Beecham's Pills! why—are you unwell?" said Mrs. Hose.

"Oh dear no, but in case of necessity," said Miss Junick, "and perhaps when I get there I may find some other things which I want to buy in the shops."

Oh certainly, you may go," said Mrs. Hose, "but you wont be back late, will you, because of Baby?"

Oh! I have put the baby to bed," said Miss Junick, cocking her head in the air, and slamming the door behind her.

7

WHAT MISS JUNICK DID IN THE TOWN

Miss Junick arrived in the town at about eight o'clock! She went straight to the Doctor's house and rang loudly at the bell. In a few minutes it was answered by a boy in buttons who asked her what she wanted, and on replying that she wanted to see the Doctor, she was shown into a neat little drawing room draped in green and red silk. Soon she heard the Doctor's bold step. He opened the door and in he came dressed in an evening suit. He bowed politely as he shut the door, saying—"Have I the pleasure of seeing Miss Junick the new and accomplished governess of Mrs. Hose?" "Yes—you have that pleasure," she said, getting up and bowing also.

And what is it you have come to ask me, Miss Junick? he said preparing to sit down in his arm chair.

Oh! she said, I have come to ask you where Mrs. Hose got her most lovely baby from.

"Oh, said the Doctor, I gave it to her because she wished for one," "Do you think you could manage to give me a baby like him?" said Miss Junick.

"Well, said the Doctor, the first question is, are you married?

"No, I am not married, but I will marry if you can give me a baby like that—it would be worth marrying for."

"Well! you cannot marry until someone asks you, and I cant because I have a wife of my own," said the Doctor.

"Well! can I have a baby like it even if I don't marry?" said Miss Junick.

"Oh well! I dont think so; Is that all you have come to ask me"? he said, in an aggravating tone, beginning to open the door for her.

"Yes, that is all," said Miss Junick, "but you will try and find a baby for me, wont you?

"Yes, but you say you are not married," said the Doctor.

"Well! I must have made a mistake, and was not thinking of what I was saying, for I certainly am".

"Oh yes, I will try and find one—Good evening Miss Junick," said the Doctor."

"Good evening Doctor Brandon, said Miss Junick, and she shut the hall door behind her, and commenced to walk up the town.

Dear dear it is nine oclock oh no half past I must hurry or Mrs. Hose will be cross and say I neglect the child and I dont only she will think so because I have it for too long only an hour and half it is not at all long. At last she came to the house and she went strait to bed but she could not sleep for thinking of the baby which she was going to have. She did not get scolded in spite of all she said.

8

THE PRIVATE ARIVAL OF MISS JUNICKS BABY

Miss Junick awoke early the next morning; she was very excited thinking of her future baby, and she didn't get up until eight o'clock. She then walked downstairs to the baby's room, and got it up. When it was dressed she gave it its breakfast, but she didn't talk to it, as much as she did the other day, for she was too much excited. After breakfast, she found it's pram in the shed and took it out for it's walk.

At last she arrived home, and after giving the baby its dinner, she put it to it's afternoon sleep. When it woke up she took it for another walk, and on her way she met the doctor's page boy coming along with a box under his arm. As she saw him approaching she left the pram without a word and ran along to meet him. When she got up to him, the boy raised his cap and said. "If you please, Miss, the doctor told me to bring you this box and he hopes the contents will do."

"Oh, thank you, thank you; " said Miss Junick, as she took the parcel, and ran back to the pram with it.

She put the box in, and walked hastily home, for she wanted to open it. Soon she got to the house, and to her great horror, as she was going upstairs she met Mrs. Hose.

"Well, Miss Junick, have you been taking baby for a walk? she said; "and what is that box you have under your arm."

"It is only something I have bought, nothing to do with you," she muttered, as Mrs. Hose shut her bedroom door.

When she had undressed the baby, she set it up in it's high chair gave it it's rattle, and hurried upstairs to open her precious box.

"I hope it's nice," she said, as she cut the string; she then opened the lid of the box. Of course it was ugly, as most babies are when they are first born.

But this would not do for Miss Junick, for she called it "an ugly little beast," and threatened to throw it away.

When the next day came she thought it was more ugly still, and that day she really did throw it away, and I will tell you where she put it."

In fact she did more than this, for she murdered it first, and then threw it into one of the dirty alleys. She was now quite satisfied that she had got rid of it, but she was more angry still when she found the bill inside the box, "Miss Junick Dr. to Doctor Paulin for one baby delivered as per agreement £1." She took the £1 out of her purse and walked straight down to the Doctors and gave it without a minutes delay and begged to have a receipt at once. So it was given to her at once, and he asked her in and cross questioned her about the baby. She paused a little and then said—

"Oh its getting on very nicely thank you, good afternoon," and she shut the outer door and hurried away home.

When she got home Mrs. Hose's baby was sleeping quietly in its cradle, but it soon woke up and she gave it is tea. Pretty soon after tea it went to bed, and she went up to her room, and I must tell you that her front window looked out upon the churchyard. She was looking out of this window as she was doing her hair, and she saw that the burial of a little baby was going on, and two poor women were there. Miss Junick pierced very hard out of the window and she recognised that it was the same little baby that she had murdered and thrown away.

"Oh! so they are burying it are they?" she said to herself, "I wouldn't take pity on such an ugly little thing if I were them."

When she had changed her dress she went downstairs to have her supper with Mr. and Mrs. Hose thinking all the while of what she had seen. When supper was over, she went upstairs and took from her trunk a "shilling shocker" and began to read it. Presently she got tired and went to bed.

9

MISS JUNICK'S PLANS

Many years had passed by since Miss Junick had come to
Mr. and Mrs. Hose, and Mrs. Hose's baby was now two
years old, and Mr. Hose was very much mastaken in what
he had said at first about Miss Junick helping them in the
evening for she did nothing but read shilling shockers
and penny horribles all the eveing till it was time for bed
and after that when she was in bed she used to make plans
these were what she maid, as she found her baby ugly and
that she could not get one like Mrs Hoses she planed
that she would steal Mrs. Hoses most lovely baby, little
did Miss Junick think that the baby she was going to steal
was the greatest tressure Mrs. Hose had ever had so she
realy planed to do this wicked act. She was very kind too
the baby all this time and each day she grew more and
more jealous of the baby and she said her plain must soon
happen and I will tell you more in the next chapter.

10

HOW MISS JUNICK CARYS OUT HER PLAN

2 weaks had past since Miss Junick had planed what she should do. One eveing she pretented too have a bad headache and went to bed before supper and had her supper in bed in order that she might think it over, yes she said I will steal the baby tomorrow and run away home to my mother and father they will be plased to know that I have stolen something and she turned on her side I will put mine and some of the babys things in a bag very early at about 5 oclock and start off so saying she began to snore and too go too sleap. soon the morning came and she awoke and dressed and hurryeld put her clothes and one dress and one cloack and bonnet of the babys in the bag and soon she and the baby were in the train for Chichester were she and her father and mother lived. The baby screamed and cried because it was tired and wanted too go to sleap but wound not because it was in the train and had never been in a train before.

Miss Junick had forgotten to bring the babys own bottel but she had a small tin of biscuits in her bag and a bottel of sour milk which she had entendid for herself but gave it too the baby because it was very hungry and had not had anything too eat since its tea the eveing before. all this time Mrs. Hose was greeving over the loss of her baby and who she thought was her dear good governess can any one have murdered them Charlie she said and buried their bodys somewere No I dont think that could have happened but we might send round to Mrs. Wight and ask her if she has seen anything of them said Charlie. Yes we will do that said Mrs. Hose, I will go and wright a note and the weping lady left the room. She soon came back I have written to Mrs. Wight she said the boy has taken the note and I expect an asew soon and she was wright for in 3 mimets the boy entered and said if you plase Mum Mrs. Wight had come to see you herself she is in the drawing room and wants you. now very well said Mrs. Hose and she walked down stairs and into the drawing room. Oh how do you do said Mrs. Wight I got your note sit down I will explain all about this. Mrs. Hose sat down and Mrs. wight began her story. Well she said I one eveing saw Miss Junick taking an eveing stroll and I asked her to come to my house and she said as you are a great friend I will tell you this so she said I am very jealous of Mrs. Hose's baby and some day I mean to steal him and run away with him and go to my own mother and father and I promised I would not say a word to anyone.

Mrs. Hose jumped up from her chair Oh Mrs. Wight if you had only told me this before I could have saved my own darling baby from been stolen from that wicked women and I will now put the blame on you. but why said Mrs. Wight I think it was very good of me to keep my promise so well.

My dear Mrs. wight said Mrs. Hose if you had told me before I could have given notice to that wicked Miss Junick and she would have left us before she could have time to steal my preschus darling and Mrs. Hose left the room and rushed upstairs to tell her husband the bad newes and Mrs. wight went home.

Mrs. hose ran into her husbands bedroom Charlie, Charlie, she said what *do* you think that wicked Miss Junick whom we thought was so good has stolen our

precious baby from us and that silly Mrs. wight new of this all along but never told us simply because Miss Junick asked her not too she new that Miss Junick was going to steal him and the words died off her lips as she fainted into a fitt Mr. Hose burnt a feather under her nose to make her come round and she soon revived and was able to say more to Mr. Hose.

MR. HOSE MAKES ENQUIRIES

Early the next morning Mr. Hose got up dressed quickly and instead of going to his office he went to the police office and made enquiries and this is what he said to inspecter have you seen a young lady with a little baby. I got a governes for my little boy and now she has stolen him and has gone home to her parents her Mother is a murderdress and her father is a robber I have no idear were her parents live, No Sir said inspecter gong I have not seen her I dont think could you dicribe her and the baby to me and then I could make sure weather I had seen her or not. Well said Mr. Hose the governess was an elderly person with sharpe black eyes and black hair and a salow complexion I do not no how she was dressed at the time for it was quite early in the morning when she stole my baby. No sir replyed inspecter Gong I have seen no such person, oh thank you said Mr. Hose good Morning, good morning Sir said the inspector as he shut the door of the police office and Mr. Hose went down the steps and walked feeling very unsatisfactory.

Many years have passed since Mr Hose lost his child Mrs
Hose had died of greef two years befor and often in the
eveing when Mr Hose sat alonne he would say to himself
would I had that wretched Miss Junick by the scraff of
the neck and he picked up the poker and shook it to show
what he would do if he had her in his hands. one eveing
as Mr. Hose sat gazeing in to the emty great where there
should have been a fire, he heard footsteps in the Porch
Mr Hose was startled for now that Mrs Hose was dead

people seldom came near the house and Mr Hose was not much to look at, he had very little hair and what he had was very seldom brushed and his red nose got bigger every day so you can emagin how few people ventured near him. when he heard the bell ring he jumped up and asked the servent who it was she said she would go and see she soon apperd and said it was a young man wanted to know if Mr Hose lived here show him in and say I do. Just at that moment a man rushed in father he said dont you know me, and he flung himself into Mr Hoses arms my son my son where have you been all theses long years tell me all about it. where is mother I must tell her too why my son you will never see your mother again she is dead she has dided for the loss of you ah I have had whom I thought was my mother and it was not untill I saw in the paper that I was still bieng looked for and that my name was Charlie Hose and Mr Hose was still alive while my supposed name was Auther Junick that I was determined to escape and so I did. well my son I cant tell you how glad I am to have you back again saying you were 1 year old when we missed you If your mother had only been here to see you safe at home and Miss Junick in Prison and always had you with her she would rejoice. and now hoping *I* have pleased I will end my story of the Jealous governess or the granted wish.